ELMHURST PUBLIC LIBRARY

3 1135 01921 1686

W9-BYZ-067

J
551.21
Col

EARTH SCIENCE DETECTIVES

Investigating
Volcanoes

ELMHURST PUBLIC LIBRARY
125 S. Prospect Avenue
Elmhurst, IL 60126-3298

Miriam Coleman

PowerKiDS press.

New York

Published in 2016 by The Rosen Publishing Group, Inc.
29 East 21st Street, New York, NY 10010

Copyright © 2016 by The Rosen Publishing Group, Inc.

All rights reserved. No part of this book may be reproduced in any form without permission in writing from the publisher, except by a reviewer.

First Edition

Editor: Sarah Machajewski
Book Design: Katelyn Heinle

Photo Credits: Cover Pablo Hidalgo/Shutterstock.com; p. 5 Ammit Jack/Shutterstock.com; p. 7 daulon/Shutterstock.com; p. 8 beboy/Shutterstock.com; p. 9 Robert Crow/Shutterstock.com; p. 10 Pichugin Dmitry/Shutterstock.com; p. 11 Tony Northrup/Shutterstock.com; p. 13 (main) http://commons.wikimedia.org/wiki/File:Bands_of_glowing_magma_from_submarine_volcano.jpg; p. 13 (inset) Vitoriano Junior/Shutterstock.com; p. 14 Henner Damke/Shutterstock.com; p. 15 Peter Hermes Furian/Shutterstock.com; p. 17 (shield volcano) Michele Falzone/Photodisc/Getty Images; p. 17 (cinder cone volcano) Chris Harris/All Canada Photos/Getty Images; p. 17 (composite volcano) suronin/Shutterstock.com; p. 18 (before) http://commons.wikimedia.org/wiki/File:Mount_St._Helens_1979.jpg; p. 18 (after) Robert Crum/Shutterstock.com; p. 19 Science Source/USGS/Science Source/Getty Images; p. 21 Photo Researchers/Science Source/Getty Images; p. 22 Suwit Gamolglang/Shutterstock.com.

Library of Congress Cataloging-in-Publication Data

Coleman, Miriam.
Investigating volcanoes / by Miriam Coleman.
p. cm. — (Earth science detectives)
Includes index.
ISBN 978-1-4777-5955-4 (pbk.)
ISBN 978-1-4777-5956-1 (6-pack)
ISBN 978-1-4777-5954-7 (library binding)
1. Volcanoes — Juvenile literature. 2. Plate tectonics — Juvenile literature. 3. Earth sciences — Juvenile literature. I. Coleman, Miriam. II. Title.
QE521.3 C65 2015
551.21—d23

Manufactured in the United States of America

CPSIA Compliance Information: Batch #WS15PK: For Further Information contact Rosen Publishing, New York, New York at 1-800-237-9932

CONTENTS

A HOT AND RESTLESS PLANET

Powerful forces beneath our feet change Earth's shape. Deep underground, heat and **pressure** are hard at work. We can't see this happening, but when volcanoes **erupt**, they **reveal** important clues about what's happening down below.

Scientists called volcanologists study volcanoes for clues about Earth. They study how volcanoes form and when they might erupt. They also study how volcanoes have changed the planet over time and how they continue to shape our world. What clues can these fiery mountains tell us about Earth's past, present, and future?

CLUE ME IN

The word "volcano" comes from Vulcan, the Roman god of fire.

This image shows Tungurahua, a volcano in Ecuador. Its name means "throat of fire."

PARTS OF A VOLCANO

A volcano is an opening in Earth's crust that allows melted rock, ash, and gases to come aboveground. A hollow tube called a vent runs from the top of the volcano down into a pool of **molten** rock, called magma.

Magma builds up in an area called a magma chamber. The magma chamber contains a lot of heat and pressure. The heat and pressure act on the magma and force it up through the vent. The melted rock, ash, and gas exit through a crater.

CLUE ME IN

Magma that comes aboveground is called lava. Lava is hot at first, but cools and hardens into a kind of rock called igneous rock.

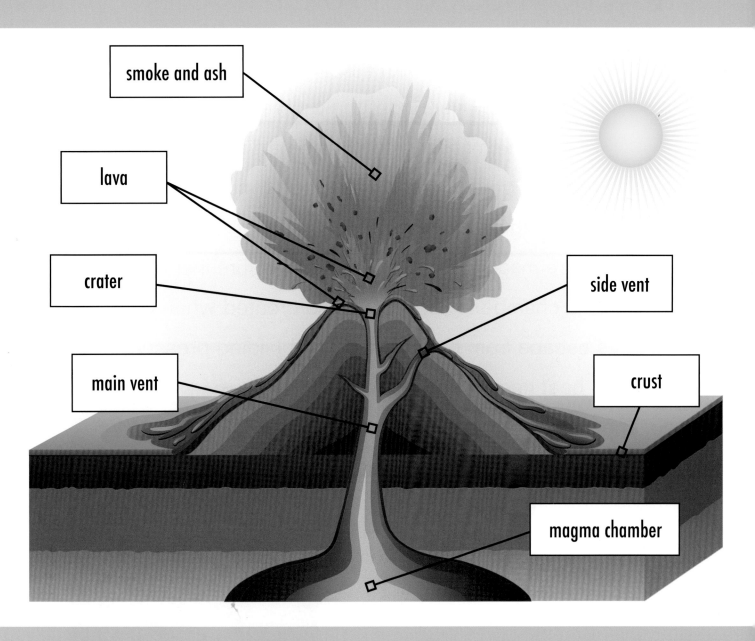

smoke and ash

lava

crater

main vent

side vent

crust

magma chamber

Many volcanoes have side vents in addition to their main vent. A side vent is an opening in the side of a volcano from which ash, gas, and lava erupt.

HOW DO VOLCANOES FORM?

Scientists separate Earth into **layers**. The rocky crust is the top layer. The layer under the crust is called the mantle. Part of the mantle is solid, and part is made of soft, flowing rock. Magma forms from the soft rock, rises, and collects in a magma chamber.

As more magma rises, it creates pressure inside the magma chamber. Pressure is also created when gas bubbles escape from the magma. The building pressure and high heat need somewhere to go. The pressure pushes magma up through the vent, where it then bursts through Earth's surface.

Cooling lava forms new land and changes Earth's **landscape**. This is just one way volcanoes affect our land.

KINDS OF MAGMA

A volcano's fiery explosion is an amazing sight. There are different kinds of lava, which come from three different kinds of magma.

Basaltic magma is the hottest type. It can reach 2,192°F (1,200°C)! When it erupts, it forms thin, flowing lava. Andesitic magma can reach 1,832°F (1,000°C). It erupts as thick lava filled with rubble, falling ash, and **pumice**.

Rhyolitic magma only reaches 1,472°F (800°C). It contains large amounts of gas and is very explosive. Volcanoes that contain this kind of magma produce very thin lava, as well as falling pumice and ash.

CLUE ME IN
The amount of gas in magma **determines** how explosive it is. More gas means a greater explosion!

What kind of magma is bubbling beneath this volcano? Scientists will only know once it erupts.

PLATES AND VOLCANOES

Scientists believe Earth's crust and upper mantle form a rocky layer that's split into giant pieces called tectonic (tehk-TAH-nihk) plates. The plates fit together like a puzzle. They float on top of the mantle's soft, flowing layer, causing them to move very slowly. They can move against or away from each other.

What does this have to do with volcanoes? Most volcanoes form at the borders between plates. When two plates move apart, magma rises up into the space between them. When two plates bump into each other, one plate is forced under the other. The lower plate partly melts to form magma, which rises through the crust.

CLUE ME IN

When two plates pull apart, the magma spills out as lava and makes a chain of volcanoes called a spreading ridge. Spreading ridges are often found along ocean floors.

plate

magma

plate

Lava that flows from an underwater volcano can be called pillow lava. The water often causes the lava to take on a pillow-like shape, as seen in the image here.

HOT, HOT, HOT!

Some volcanoes form in the middle of plates instead of at their boundaries. They're caused by hot spots—very hot areas deep within the mantle. Hot spots melt the rock in the plate above them, creating large amounts of magma. The magma rises up, breaks through the surface, and forms volcanoes.

A hot spot stays in the same place while the plate above it moves. This means the same hot spot can create a chain of volcanoes. One hot spot formed all the Hawaiian Islands! Each undersea volcano produced enough magma to rise and form an island before the plate moved and a new volcano began.

Haleakalā on the island of Maui is just one of Hawaii's many volcanoes.

CLUE ME IN

The Hawaiian hot spot has been creating volcanoes for about 70 million years. The chain of volcanoes it's produced is over 3,100 miles (5,000 km) long!

Kauai

Niihau

PACIFIC OCEAN

Oahu

Molokai

Maui

Lanai

PACIFIC OCEAN

Kahoolawe

HAWAII

Hawaii

The Hawaiian Islands and their volcanoes are **evidence** that a hot spot exists under the Pacific Ocean—and that the plate resting on it is moving.

KINDS OF VOLCANOES

Looking at the shape of a volcano can tell scientists a lot about how it erupts. Cinder cone volcanoes erupt thick blobs of lava and rock out of their bowl-shaped crater. The materials land and cool near the opening, forming a steep-sided cone.

Shield volcanoes are broad mounds with gentle slopes. They form when thin lava flows out of a vent and spreads over a wide area. Shield volcanoes can grow to be several miles across. Composite volcanoes erupt flowing lava as well as violent explosions of ash, cinders, and rock. These different materials build up in layers and form steep-sided cones.

CLUE ME IN
Two of the world's most active volcanoes, Kilauea and Mauna Loa in Hawaii, are shield volcanoes.

cinder cone volcano

composite volcano

shield volcano

Cinder cone volcanoes rarely reach over 1,000 feet (305 m). Some shield volcanoes are huge. Mauna Loa rises almost 14,000 feet (4,267 m) above sea level! Composite volcanoes can rise to be as tall as 8,000 feet (2,438 m).

EXTREME ERUPTIONS

Volcanoes are very **dangerous** when they erupt. Hot, flowing lava can destroy everything in its path. Lava isn't the only thing to worry about, though. Pyroclastic (py-roh-KLAS-tihk) flows, or fast-moving mixtures of very hot gas and rock, are even worse. They can knock down and bury anything nearby and set forests and buildings on fire. Volcanoes can also set off dangerous mudflows and **landslides**.

Mount St. Helens before

Mount St. Helens after

Volcanoes have changed Earth's landscape many times over. The eruption of Mount St. Helens in 1980 damaged 230 square miles (596 sq km) of land around it, including cities, water, and forests, and killed plants and animals that lived nearby.

Falling ash can bury farms and destroy crops. When ash and gases from eruptions fill the sky, they can block out the sun and even change the **climate** around the world.

SEEKING CLUES IN VOLCANOES

Volcanoes can be very destructive, so scientists look for clues that a volcano is getting ready to blow. There are three main warning signs. An increase in earthquakes around a volcano can mean magma is moving toward the surface. Gas is another clue. If the gases get hotter or more gas is released, it can mean a volcano is preparing to erupt.

Scientists also watch a volcano's shape. When magma rises, it pushes on the rocks around it. Huge **bulges** growing quickly on mountainsides are good clues that an explosion may happen soon.

CLUE ME IN

An active volcano is one that erupts regularly. A dormant volcano is one that hasn't erupted in a while, but could in the future. An extinct volcano is one that will never erupt again.

These volcanologists study volcanoes to learn what's happening below Earth's surface. Finding and recognizing warning signs can help people prepare for an explosion.

LEARNING ABOUT EARTH

Volcanologists have many ways of studying volcanoes. They look at the land around them to learn about past eruptions. They measure earthquake activity and **temperature** changes. They climb the slopes of volcanoes to study how the ground has changed, and they climb into craters to study where lava flow begins. They collect samples of rocks, and they study the ashes that explode from Earth.

Especially brave scientists study hot lava. They wear special suits to protect them from the heat. Studying volcanoes can be dangerous, but it provides important clues about what goes on far below Earth's surface.

GLOSSARY

bulge: A rounded swelling produced by pressure.

climate: The weather in an area over a period of time.

dangerous: Not safe.

determine: To cause something to occur in a particular way.

erupt: To become active and send out lava, ash, and gases.

evidence: Facts, signs, or information that proves something to be true.

landscape: The features of an area of land.

landslide: The sliding down of a mass of earth or rock from a mountain or cliff.

layer: One thickness lying over or under another.

molten: Melted by heat.

pressure: A force that pushes on something else.

pumice: A very light volcanic rock.

reveal: To make known.

temperature: How hot or cold something is.

INDEX

WEBSITES

Due to the changing nature of Internet links, PowerKids Press has developed an online list of websites related to the subject of this book. This site is updated regularly. Please use this link to access the list: www.powerkidslinks.com/det/volc